a fishy coat
and other poems

Diana Moore

First published in 2012

ISBN 978-1-4681-8055-8

How many tales in this book could be true?
Some parts are fact, I will leave it to you

a fishy coat tale
and other poems

leona leopard says...

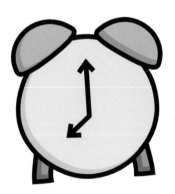

Every morning when I rise
I count the spots before my eyes
Starting left, I work clockwise
And are they all of equal size?

If I offered you a prize
To come much closer and surmise
The total spots before your eyes

Do you think it would be wise…?

jackdaw

Good morning Jack
With the noisy *chack*
Chack chack chacking
In the chimney stacking

Arriving in
Diving in
I'm not alive in
The morning at five
As you are

And Jack,
You know it's not the best idea
To nest here
You could choke
On fireside smoke

Caw! Caw! Do I have to go?

You know you do

Jack *chack*
Jack *chack*
Jack *chack*
Flap flap flap
Your wings and go...

Along came the sweep
With his brush on a stick
He scraped out the debris
Of soot - it was thick

Out with the twigs
Out with the straw
Out with the wool
Out with the caw caw calling
In the morning

Out with the back chat
Jack

And Jack flew off

But then he flew back

He peck peck pecked
At the grid of wire
He tug tug tugged at the wired frame

Kow kow kow
How how how do I get in?

Kow kow kow
How how how do I get in?

He peck peck peck peck pecked
Vexed

He peck peck peck peck pecked
Perplexed

And Jack flew off

No more caw caw calling
In the chimney cowling

blossom's tale

Do you know there's a mouse
Who sneaks into my hutch
He jumps into my food bowl
He doesn't eat much

He asked the other evening
He asked me with a 'please'
Would I ask my owner
For a bit of cheese

three fine lice

Three fine lice, three fine lice
See how they run, see how they run
They all ran over to Harry's head
Nestled down in his hair like a bedspread
Then fled in dread at the silicone spread
Those three fine lice

a fishy coat tale

All fish love
to wear a coat

Whether swimming
sea or moat

Trout, a housecoat
soft and sheer

Pollock chooses
fine cashmere

11

Stingray loves
electric blue

Mullet craves
a golden hue

The eel, a blazer
striped with pink

While dace is shunned
for wearing mink

A tiny little minnow's whim

Is black and shiny with fur trim

A perch delights
in gabardine

A mohaired cod
creates a scene…

15

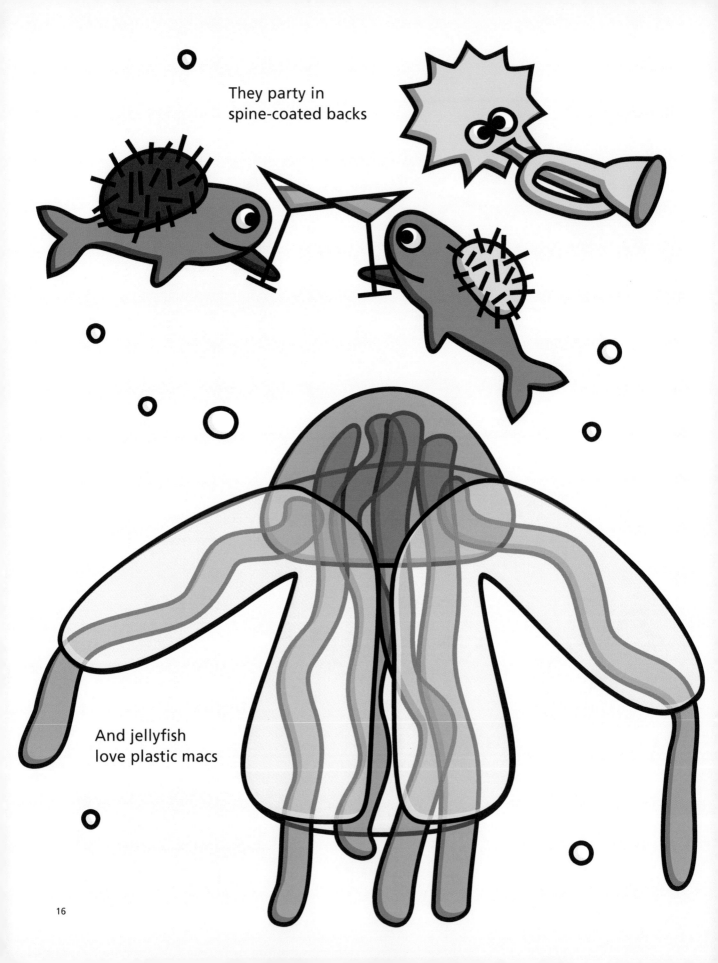

They party in
spine-coated backs

And jellyfish
love plastic macs

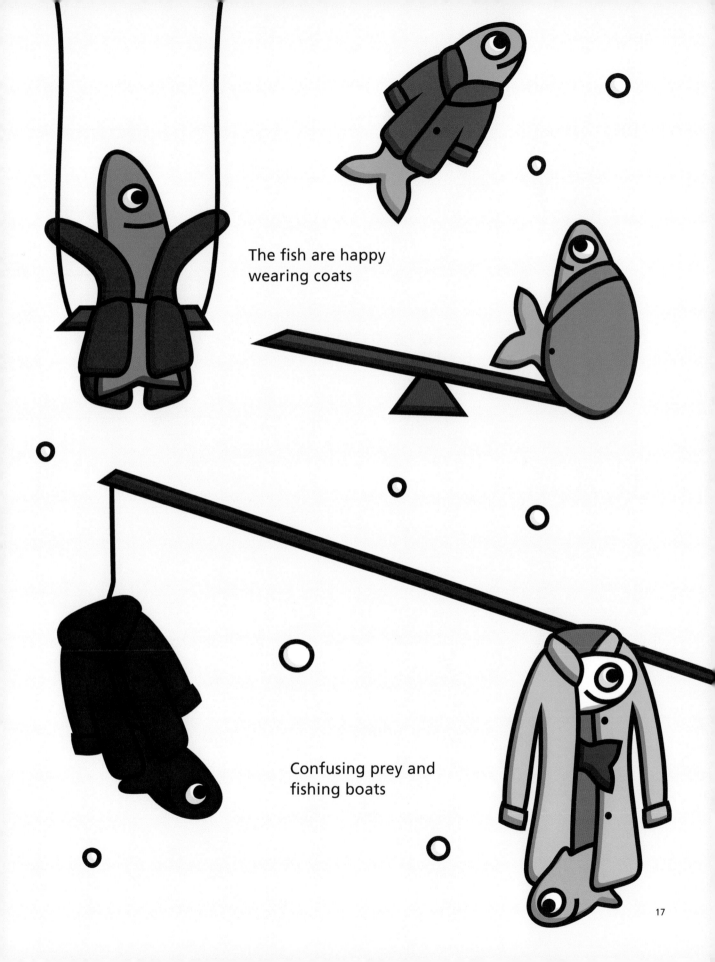

The fish are happy
wearing coats

Confusing prey and
fishing boats

17

flyway code

"Crossing country roads is a nightmare", cried pheasant
"My timing could be wrong and the outcome... unpleasant"

horsewife

When no one is looking
I put on a pinny
I cook oaty flapjacks
And let out a whinny

a stable song for horse lovers
(to the tune of frères jacques)

Grassy dumplings
Grassy dumplings
In a heap
In a heap
Throw them out the stable
Throw them out the stable
What a pong
Ding dang dong

Fetch the straw bales
Fetch the straw bales
Spread them out
Spread them out
Horsey has a clean home
Horsey has a clean home
No more smells
Ring the bells

molly the dog

Molly has a poorly paw
She cannot leap out of the door
Her daily walkies are no more
Molly can't be Jolly

Molly Molly loves her ball
Leaping high and running free
When she's fit she'll roam with me
And Molly can be jolly

"I need to chase my tennis ball
My strength is as a fetcher
Is there any chance at all
Of walkies on a stretcher?"

cornelia cat and dimitri dog audition for tchaikovsky's 'the nutcracker'

(overture - march)

Meow woofety meow meow
Woof woof meow
Meow woofety meow meow
Woof woof meow

Meow meow woof woofy woof
Meow meow woof woofy woof

Meow woof woof
Meow woof woof
Meowly howly growl hiss!

Meow woofety meow meow
Woof woof meow
Meow woofety meow meow
Woof woof meow

Meow meow woof woofy woof
Meow meow woof woofy woof

Woof woofety woof woofety meow meow meow grrr!

Meow woofety meow meow woof woof howl
Meow meow meow meow meow meow meow meow woof

Meow woofety meow meow woof woof howl

Meow meow meow meow meow meow meow
Woof woof woof woof-woof-woof

REPEAT FROM TOP

the frog and the birthday girl

There was a young lady called Sue
Who encountered a dashing frog - ooh!
"Birthday girl" sung the frog
Hop this way for a snog
And their love on a lily pad grew

But the frog had a rival called Stu
Who raced on his bike to fetch Sue
He reached the lagoon
By the light of the moon
And demanded of froggy "Don't woo!"

Now froggy was one in a million
His cheeks turned the brightest vermillion
Said he: "Stu, you have won
Now I wonder, for fun,
Could I travel with you on your pillion?"

Sue felt for the frog a deep liking
For his features were notably striking
They agreed *Harley D*
Could cope with all three
And set off through the woods motor biking

The wind caught frog's hair and it flowed
By the silvery moonlight he glowed
As the engine grew hotter
Froggy turned terra cotta
And resembled an earthenware toad

23

mary had a mobile phone

Mary had a mobile phone
She gave it to her lamb
The lamb recorded dancing sheep
And shared it on 'lamb cam'

The sheep received a call
To do the rumba on TV
They signed a contract for a film
And Sheep Songs DVD

The sheep do gigs and shows
With light and sound that is amazing
But mostly they prefer to keep
Their quiet life of grazing

Printed in Poland
by Amazon Fulfillment
Poland Sp. z o.o., Wrocław